Mindful Metrics
Analytics for the Reflective Marketer

Table of Contents

Chapter 1. Introduction

Is it possible to navigate the world of digital marketing not just proficiently, but also mindfully? The answer is a resounding yes! Welcome to 'Mindful Metrics: Analytics for the Reflective Marketer'. This Special Report is your answer to combining efficiency and empathy in your marketing strategy. You'll learn how to transform data into perceptive insights about your customers, view analytics through the lens of ethical responsiveness, and make marketing feel less like a battle, and more like a mindful dialogue. But it's not just about nurturing your clients; it's also about refining your marketing acumen. No need for coding prowess or an advanced degree! This guide walks you through the process step-by-step with simple language and clear examples. If you're ready to turn raw data into relationship-building insights and foster a more mindful balance in your marketing role, get your hands on this transformative guide today!

Chapter 2. Demystifying Metrics: The Basics

Metrics, in the realm of digital marketing, act as the backbone of your strategy, providing. Despite their undeniable importance, they are often misunderstood or misinterpreted by marketers. This chapter guides you through the maze of marketing metrics, offering a comprehensive understanding of their function, relevance, and use.

2.1. The Fundamental Foundations

To start, let us delve into the three significant types of metrics that marketers utilize: Vanity, Engagement, and ROI metrics.

Vanity Metrics often give a feel-good factor as they showcase numbers like total followers, website visits, or downloads. While these may seem impressive, they seldom provide an insight into the quality of those interactions or how they contribute to your business goals.

Engagement Metrics look beyond the surface and try to understand the depth of the interaction. Engagement metrics, including likes, comments, shares, average time on page, and click-through rates, show how audiences interact with your content.

ROI Metrics quantify the return on investment for your marketing efforts. They include conversion rates, cost per click (CPC), cost per acquisition (CPA), and customer lifetime value (CLV).

Understanding these categories helps marketers track and interpret the right metrics, linking marketing efforts closer to business goals.

2.2. Embracing the Power of Key Performance Indicators

Key Performance Indicators (KPIs) are a marketer's compass, guiding the strategy. They help quantify goals, set benchmarks, and track progress. Essentially, KPIs make your marketing endeavours measurable.

When choosing KPIs, reflect on your organization's specific goals and context. Do you want to increase brand awareness, drive conversions, or foster customer loyalty? Once you identify these goals, you can designate corresponding KPIs.

Remember, your KPIs might change as your strategy evolves, and that's okay. It's part of the dynamic nature of digital marketing, allowing you to be responsive and adaptive.

2.3. Diving Deeper: Understanding Analytics Tool

Now that we've established a foundation, let's uncover the various tools to track and analyse metrics. Google Analytics is a dominating presence in this arena, offering numerous tracking options catering to every marketing goal you might have.

Understanding Google Analytics extends beyond the scope of this chapter. However, a cursory overview will help you realize its potential:

- **Audience Overview Report**: Provides demographics, user behaviour, and technology preferences of your audience.

- **Acquisition Report**: Tells you where your traffic comes from.

- **Behaviour Report**: Highlights how users interact with your site.

- **Conversion Report**: Outlines how successful you are at achieving your predetermined goals.

These tools can provide real-time insights into your marketing efforts. Adapt your strategy according to these reports to maximise your impact.

2.4. Metrics in Practice: Case Studies

To cement your understanding, let's learn from marketers in action. Some of the biggest brands have used metrics to transform their approach. A deep dive into these successful case studies will show you the expansive potential of metrics.

Netflix uses metrics to understand viewing habits and personalise recommendations. This practice has increased viewer engagement and reduced churn rate.

Airbnb analyses metrics to identify popular destinations and optimise their listings accordingly. This proactive use of metrics helps the company stay ahead in a competitive market.

2.5. Final Reflections: A Mindful Approach to Metrics

The journey through marketing metrics is certainly challenging, but with mindfulness, it can be rewarding. Reflect on your goals, choose your KPIs wisely, and let the metrics guide your strategy.

By doing so, you'll create a marketing strategy that's not only effective but also empathetic. This empathetic approach helps you connect more deeply with your customers, fostering long-term relationships.

With the insights you've gained from this chapter, you're well on your way to creating a marketing strategy that is mindful, responsive, and metric-driven. Become more than a marketer; be a navigator, led by the compass of metrics and readiness to adapt to new knowledge.

Remember, the journey of digital marketing is an ongoing process, requiring consistent learning, questioning, and refining. You're cultivating not only a better understanding of metrics but also a broader appreciation for the narrative they weave about your audience and your brand.

Chapter 3. The Reflective Marketer: An Introduction

Marketing, as a role, is often equated to strategizing, promoting, and selling, but the duties of a modern-day marketer go far beyond these familiar spheres. Today, marketing incorporates a deep understanding of data, gleaning insights from it, and establishing a connection with your customers based on obtained information. It is where mindfulness and metrics converge in the orchestration of strategies, leading to what we coined here as the 'Reflective Marketer', who doesn't merely sell, but enriches lives.

3.1. The Era of Customer Experience

In this digitally-dominated world, the customer is firmly in the driver's seat, dictating preference trends and continually transforming their buying behavior. Contrary to the traditional ways, marketing today is less about pushing products or services and more about delivering impressive customer experiences. In this sense, marketers have evolved into caretakers of the customer journey, focusing on creating and enhancing customer interactions throughout the full marketing funnel.

Consider the data - according to a Walker study, by 2020, customer experience has overtaken price and product as the key brand differentiator. Hence, curating an exceptional customer experience has become the 'be-all and end-all' of contemporary marketing strategies.

3.2. Understanding Data and Analytics

To succeed in the experience-centric market, marketers need to understand their customers on a profound level. Data and analytics play crucial roles in this context, providing insights into customer characteristics and behaviors.

Data analytics gives you access to an invaluable commodity - actionable intelligence. By thoroughly scrutinizing data, marketers can determine customer preferences, anticipate needs, and predict behaviors. These insights can help craft personalized experiences, reduce customer churn, and fuel revenue growth.

3.3. The Reflective Marketer: Merging Mindfulness with Metrics

Being a 'Reflective Marketer' denotes incorporating a level of mindfulness into strategy design and decision making. It involves a conscious consideration of both the measurable and immeasurable components of marketing and making well-rounded, enlightened decisions.

Reflective marketing involves three essential elements:

1. Empathetic Engagement: Understand and connect with your clients on a deeper emotional level.

2. Ethical Responsiveness: Guided by values, take actions that consider your customer's best interests.

3. Evolutionary Instinct: Continually adapt to the ever-changing marketing landscape and customer behaviors.

3.4. Empathetic Engagement

Making empathy a significant part of your marketing strategy transforms the way you connect with your customers. Rather than viewing customers as revenue generators, empathetic engagement revolves around understanding customers as individual beings with diverse needs and preferences.

This approach demands that you look beyond data and analytics and attempt to comprehend the human aspect of information. It necessitates a more profound focus on individual customer journeys, understanding their concerns, and genuinely taking steps to address them.

3.5. Ethical Responsiveness

Ethical responsiveness in marketing means that your practices and decisions consider the best interests of customers and respect their rights at all levels. This approach is fundamental for creating a brand that customers trust. Trust, once gained, fosters loyalty, and loyalty leads to ongoing customer engagement and long-term revenue.

3.6. Evolutionary Instinct

The 'Reflective Marketer' must continually adapt to shifts in the marketing landscape. Adapting does not merely mean embracing new technology, but rather understanding the underlying changes in customer behavior, needs, and expectations that have driven such evolved trends.

The Evolutionary Instinct also pertains to learning and evolving from feedback and failures. It involves being open to learning from experiences and making continual improvements.

3.7. Conclusion

A true 'Reflective Marketer' seeks to understand customers, engage with them empathetically and ethically, and continually evolve to enrich and improve customer experiences. It is through this union of mindfulness and metrics that marketing becomes not a distraction or an interruption but an enriching dialogue between the brand and the customer.

This ethos of the 'Reflective Marketer' forms the foundation of succeeding chapters, where we will delve deeper into concrete tactics, practical strategies, and in-depth case studies. By the time you turn over the last page, you'll be well-versed with the realm of mindful metric-based marketing, ready to foster meaningful connections, enhance customer experience, and ultimately, drive your brand toward measurable success.

Chapter 4. Culture of Empathy: Understanding Your Audience

The path to crafting an impactful marketing message begins with understanding your audience in a profound, empathetic way. This holistic approach incorporates both statistical and qualitative insights to tap into the heart of your audience's needs, values, and experiences.

4.1. Building an Empathetic Framework

A foundation of empathy allows marketers to see beyond cold, detached statistics and dive into a vibrant world of unique human experiences. The development of empathy, in fact, fosters a symbiotic relationship: as marketers become more attuned to their audience's feelings and perspectives, they simultaneously enhance their capacity to develop more meaningful, compelling campaigns.

This empathy-driven approach rests upon three cornerstones: Observing, Contextualizing, and Internalizing.

Observing requires careful attention to your audience's verbal and non-verbal cues. Contextualizing involves understanding these observations within the larger landscape of the audience's life, needs, and desires. Internalizing requires stepping into the shoes of your customers, engaging with their experiences deeply, and eliciting emotional reactions similar to those they feel.

4.2. Integrating Empathy into Data Analysis

Data analysis entails more than simply tabulating numbers and plotting trends. It necessitates the application of an empathetic lens to interpret data correctly and generate nuanced insights.

An empathetic marketer will view data as a collection of individual narratives, as opposed to impersonal statistics. This perspective helps identify the audience's distinctive needs, desires, and frustrations, converting charts and graphs into a comprehensible map of the customer's journey.

Moreover, this approach aids in identifying potential pain points that might have been overlooked in a more traditional analysis. By integrating empathy into data analysis, marketers can attune their strategies to their audience's real-world needs and experiences, thereby enhancing the effectiveness and authenticity of their messages.

4.3. Enriching Audience Personas with Empathy

Empathy provides the depth and nuance necessary to bring audience personas to life. These personas embody the range of emotions, aspirations, and challenges your typical customers might experience.

Rather than just identifying demographics, a marketing persona traced with empathy will explore the emotional landscape of your audience. It might include their joys, fears, aspirations, and frustrations. By breathing life into these personas, marketers can create more resonant narratives and strategically target their messaging.

4.4. Harnessing the Power of Empathetic Storytelling

Successful marketing creates meaningful connections between brands and their audiences. Empathetic storytelling ensures these connections are deep, emotional, and authentic.

With this approach, marketers look to create narratives that resonate with their audience on a visceral level. Stories that stir emotions, trigger empathy, and bring about a sense of shared experience transcend mere transactions to forge a genuine bond between brand and audience.

4.5. Moving beyond Transactional Interactions

Too often, companies view their relationship with customers as purely transactional. However, empathy enables marketers to form meaningful bonds that go beyond a simple exchange of goods or services.

When a brand deepens its connection with customers by acknowledging their hopes, addressing their fears, and celebrating their victories, it fosters loyalty and boosts engagements. This shift from transactions to relationships can have profound implications for a brand's long-term success.

In conclusion, the shift towards empathetic marketing does not negate the importance of hard data. Instead, it augments quantitative insights with a qualitative understanding of the audience's world. It allows marketers to communicate in a language that customers truly understand, thereby enhancing engagement and fostering long-term loyalty.

In the land of marketing, statistics might guide you, but empathy will light up your path, transforming your journey from a marketing grind to a human adventure.

Chapter 5. From Numbers to Narratives: Transforming Data into Insights

Simply stated, data exists in raw figures, tables, and numbers. It's often hard to digest and even harder to turn into a narrative that can be understood by a broader audience. That's where the transformation from numbers to narratives comes into play. It involves interpreting the data, drawing sensible conclusions, and then presenting them in such a way that it communicates a story to your audience – a story that fosters understanding, empathy, and a desire to act.

5.1. Unraveling the Raw Data

It all starts with the raw data. As a marketer, you likely have access to vast amounts of data collected from various sources such as website cookies, customer surveys, social media analytics, or sales metrics. This data may look like a jumble of numbers, but with the right approach, it represents a goldmine of insights.

Begin by outlining what you know about this data: where it was sourced from, how it was gathered, and any relevant demographic information. Next, organize the data in a way that makes sense. This could be chronological, thematic, or based on consumer behaviours or patterns. Just ensure it's in a format conducive to more in-depth analysis.

5.2. The Art of Interpretation

Once you've organized the data, begin interpreting it. Start by identifying trends or patterns that appear in the data. For instance, if you notice a surge in web traffic on the weekends or that a certain demographic prefers mobile over desktop, these can lead to impactful insights. However, interpretation is not merely about observation; it's also about hypothesizing why these trends are occurring and corroborating these hypotheses with more data or research.

At times, data may contradict each other or may present confounding insights that are difficult to interpret. In such situations, additional data sources, experiments, or stakeholder interviews may help clear up the confusion.

5.3. Crafting the Narrative

Once you've interpreted the data and drawn conclusions, the next step is to weave those insights into a narrative. This is where your creative skills come into play. Use the conclusions to form the basis of your story, ensure that the narrative is clear, concise, and compelling.

First explain the context – who are the characters (audience), what are their challenges (pain points from data), and what are actions taken (consumer behaviour). You then narrate the change/transformation witnessed and finally explain the outcome, showcasing the impact your product or service had on them as evident from the data.

5.4. Visualization for Better Understanding

A crucial part of data storytelling involves visualization. Graphs, charts, infographics, and diagrams can replace convoluted data tables, making the information more digestible, highlighting important trends, and instantly capturing audience attention.

Visuals should always amplify the narrative. It's not just about creating a pretty image but providing a visual detail to your story. Tools like Google Data Studio, Tableau, or Canva have pre-set templates that can help you design compelling data visualizations, even if you don't have a background in graphic design.

5.5. The Ethics of Data Storytelling

Just as with any tool or strategy, there's a responsibility that comes with telling a data story. The narrative you craft should be based on proven data and not manipulated to fit a preconceived notion or marketing pitch.

Transparency is key in establishing trust with your audience. Let them know where your data comes from, why it was collected, and how it's being utilized. Moreover, adhere to the privacy and data protection regulations to blend ethical responsiveness in your analytics approach.

Transforming data from numbers to a narrative requires bridging the technical with the creative, the logical with the emotional. It's about finding the human stories within a sea of statistical information. So, take your raw data, interpret it thoughtfully, weave it into a story that resonates, and present it in a way that captivates. Not only will your data become more empathetic and engaging, but it can also lead to more effective and mindful marketing.

Chapter 6. Ethical Analytics: The Convergence of Profit and Principles

Analytics – the exhilarating universe of data, metrics, and charts – is a marketer's playground. It's also a landscape rich with ethical challenges. As personalization skyrockets and web tracking tools grow more sophisticated, it's vital that marketers walk this balance beam with care, combining the pursuit of profit with a commitment to ethical principles.

6.1. What is Ethical Analytics?

Contrary to a common misconception, ethical analytics isn't about compromising on your marketing goals, nor is it just about legal compliance. Ethical analytics can be seen as the intersection where efficacy and empathy meet. It's about mindfully understanding what your data represents – the people behind those numbers, their desires, their lives, and their sensitivities. An ethical approach to analytics entails a fusion of profit and principles, a blend of commercial goals and respect for consumer autonomy. In essence, this path goes beyond what you can do with your data to what you should do.

6.2. Fundamentals of Ethical Analytics

While every organization and individual will have a unique approach, there are certain universal principles to consider when diving into ethical analytics. Let's unpack these aspects:

- **Transparency:** Consumers need to know what they are signing up for. Ensure your terms, conditions, and data policies are clear, understandable, and available. With transparency comes trust, and with trust come long-term, loyal customers.

- **Informed Consent:** Related to transparency is the concept of informed consent. It's one thing to have a policy in place, but quite another to ensure your customers understand it. Implement tools and measures that ensure users know exactly what they agree to.

- **Minimal Data Collection:** Keep your data collection to the minimum necessary data. More data doesn't always translate into more insights. Collecting more than you need not only clutters your analysis but can also infringe on your customers' privacy.

- **Secure Data Storage and Handling:** Protecting your consumers' data from breaches is essential. Regular audits, secure storage systems, and limited data access are just a few ways to heighten your data security.

- **Data Anonymization and Aggregation:** Identifiable personal data is a hot-button issue. Whenever possible, anonymize and aggregate data. This will help protect identities while still allowing you to draw beneficial insights.

6.3. Balancing Business Goals and Ethical Practices

Some marketers fear that focusing on ethical analytics may hamper business performance. Yet businesses can gain tangible benefits from this approach. Ethical analytics can foster consumer trust, which translates into higher retention rates and loyalty. Improved brand image and reputation also often follow suit.

Business goals and ethical practices can coexist harmoniously, but striking this balance isn't always simple. It requires continuous effort, active listening to your audience, and an unwavering commitment to keep their best interests at the center of your marketing strategy.

6.4. Implementing Ethical Analytics in Your Marketing Strategy

Mapping out a pathway to ethical analytics can be challenging, particularly when it's new terrain. Here are key steps to guide your journey:

1. **Define Clear Objectives:** Understand what you want to achieve with your data, and let these objectives guide your data collection.

2. **Set Up Boundaries:** Clearly define what data you absolutely need, and respect the boundaries that this creates.

3. **Establish Robust Security Measures:** Invest in strong, reliable storage solutions, and routinely test and update your security systems.

4. **Keep Your Team Trained and Informed:** Regular training sessions and updates regarding changes in privacy laws or industry specific guidelines can keep the entire marketing team aligned.

5. **Monitor and Improve:** Ethical analytics is not a one-time task. Regularly assess your strategies to ensure you're maintaining ethical standards.

6.5. Ethical Analytics as an Ongoing Dialogue

If there's one takeaway from this chapter, let it be that ethical analytics is an ongoing commitment rather than a one-time project.

This dialogue between you, your customers, your data, and your ethical standards will require constant restructuring, reassessments, and realignments. But from this proactive conversation will arise not just better profits, but better principles, leading your digital marketing strategy towards mindful metrics and a reflective approach.

Chapter 7. Algorithmic Analysis for the Ethically-minded Marketer

To begin with, it's crucial to understand why algorithmic analysis is indispensable in modern digital marketing. Gone are the days when intuition and creativity alone could steer a marketing campaign. In our digitized world, data is the new oil. It fuels decision-making, drives customer insights, and informs strategic planning. With a myriad of touchpoints, from social media and email to SEO and e-commerce, marketers are inundated with data. Processing this sea of information manually is nearly impossible.

However, algorithms step in here to save the day. These mathematical formulas can quickly sift through voluminous data, detect patterns, make predictions, and provide actionable insights. Yet, algorithm-driven analysis isn't solely about crunching numbers. It's a means to a more empathetic, ethical, and efficacious marketing strategy.

7.1. The Ethics of Algorithmic Analysis

Algorithms might seem far removed from the realm of ethics, but that's a dogged misbelief. Data privacy and consent, bias and fairness, transparency and accountability – these ethical concerns are intertwined with algorithmic analysis. As marketers, becoming aware of these aspects is our first step towards a more mindful practice.

For example, consider the issue of bias. An algorithm is only as unbiased as the data it's fed. If the input data lacks diversity or holds inherent prejudices, the algorithm will reflect these in its output. This isn't just an ethical lapse—it's bad for business. An e-commerce algorithm showing women's clothing to men because it predominantly collected data from female shoppers? That's lost potential revenue.

Another critical element is data privacy. With sweeping regulations like the GDPR and CCPA, it's never been so essential for marketers to respect user consent, anonymize data, and safeguard privacy.

7.2. From Raw Data to Empathetic Insights

How can we transform raw data into empathetic insights? This isn't about manipulating data to 'appear' ethical; it's about genuinely considering the user behind the numbers. Algorithms, especially those backed by artificial intelligence (AI), can help us here.

For instance, sentiment analysis can help us perceive a customer's underlying feelings. Imagine a customer left a 3-star review but made positive comments about the product. A plain algorithm might categorize this into 'neutral', missing the sentiment complexity. An AI-driven algorithm, on the other hand, can recognize the positivity and provide a nuanced understanding.

Personalization can serve as another example. Too much personalization can feel invasive, too little may seem impersonal. Algorithms can ensure we strike the right balance, combining data from various sources to present tailored yet respectful messaging.

7.3. Tools for Ethical Algorithmic Analysis

Let's look at a few tools aiding ethical algorithmic analysis:

1. Open-Source R and Python Libraries: R's 'ethics' package, Python's 'fairlearn' and 'aif360' libraries provide fairness metrics to assess your algorithms.

2. Differential Privacy Tools: Companies like Google and Apple offer differential privacy tools to anonymize data without losing its usability.

3. AI Ethics Toolkits: Ethics-related frameworks, like IBM's AI Fairness 360 and Google's What-If Tool, can also be useful.

7.4. Ensuring a Mindful Balance in Marketing

A vibrant marketing strategy doesn't revolve around relentless selling. Rather, it's about meaningful, reciprocal dialogues with the customers. True, algorithms help us process data, but we're the ones steering their use.

So, let's commit to a mindful balance in our sphere, using our algorithmic analysis power responsibly. Privacy, fairness, transparency, accountability—let's simply ensure our algorithms align with these markers.

To conclude, the ethically-minded marketer isn't an oxymoron. In fact, bridging the gap between algorithmic efficiency and ethical mindfulness is the need of the hour. Harness your data responsibly and transform those raw numbers into empathetic, ethical, and effective insights.

Chapter 8. Mindful Connections: Relationship-Building with Metrics

Let's dive into the heart of our approach: Building mindful connections with your audience using data analytics. In the digital landscape, data can often feel impersonal or even alienating. However, when approached with a thoughtful and understanding mindset, these metrics can become a source of deep connection and communication with your audience.

8.1. Bringing Empathy into Analytics

One of the most important aspects of creating a mindful marketing strategy is the inclusion of empathy in the analysis and use of data. In the world of marketing, it's easy to forget that behind every click, like, share, comment, or page view, there is a person with their own reasons for interacting with your content.

By remembering to view the data collected not just as numbers, but as indicators of peoples' desires, frustrations, needs, and hopes, we can gain a deeper understanding of our audience. This allows us to meet them where they are and tailor our content to be more relevant and beneficial to them.

Empathy in analytics can be employed in a variety of ways. For instance, by analyzing user behavior on your website or social media pages, you can identify points where users may be experiencing frustration or confusion. This could be a page with a high bounce rate, a frequently abandoned shopping cart, or a post with a high number of negative reactions.

Rather than viewing these as failures, we can use them as

opportunities for improvement. By empathizing with users' struggles and striving to understand what they are experiencing, we can make positive changes to benefit both the user and our marketing strategy.

8.2. Transform Relationship-Building through Data

It's time to see data not merely as impersonal numbers on a chart but as a tool for deep, meaningful connection. Using data effectively can help you respond to your audience's needs and, in turn, enhance your brand's performance and relationship with your customers.

The big question to answer here is - How exactly do you do that?

This process often involves segmenting your audience based on various factors such as demographics, browsing behavior, purchase history, lifestyle interests, and more. These segments can then be used to tailor content and ads to suit each group's unique needs and preferences.

It's not enough to know your average user – you have to understand the range of individuals who make up your user base. And this takes us right back to being mindful in our approach because being aware and appreciative of the diversity in your audience is the crux of being mindful.

8.3. The Art of Listening through Analytics

Analytics is more than just measurement—it's a way of listening to your audience. Reviewing website metrics, social media interactions, product reviews, and customer feedback are all ways of hearing what your audience is saying.

While it's important to measure the success of your marketing campaigns, it's equally (if not more) important to understand why a campaign was successful or why it missed the mark. Going through customer feedback often reveals the reasons behind certain behaviors. This understanding contributes to making meaningful changes to your strategy and improving your relationship with your customers.

8.4. Balancing the Quantitative and Qualitative

While numbers provide measurable results and help capture performance, the story behind these numbers is also significant. While quantitative data shows you what is happening, qualitative data can tell you why it is happening.

This means pairing your analytics with sources of qualitative insights such as customer surveys, one-on-one interviews, focus groups, and more. This enriches your understanding of your customers and allows for a more comprehensive, empathetic approach.

8.5. Analytics for Connection, Not Just Conversion

While conversions are often a primary target in digital marketing strategies, it is important to understand that there is more to relationships than merely converting a potential customer into a buyer.

Conversion rate optimization is definitely important. But your marketing metrics should also be used to improve the overall experience of your users, promoting long-term loyalty and building trust with your audience.

Understanding the customer journey, and using analytics to refine that journey, can make the marketing experience feel less like a sales pitch and more like a dialogue between your brand and your audience.

In conclusion, embracing a mindful approach to marketing metrics has powerful potential. By viewing data analysis through the lens of empathy, mapping metrics to meaningful changes, and focusing on relationship-building over mere conversion, we can transform the digital marketing landscape. It's all about crafting a strategy that values connection, communication, and understanding above all else. In the process, we're not only building stronger relationships with our audience but also nurturing a more balanced and fulfilling marketing role for ourselves.

Chapter 9. Strategies for Implementing Reflective Marketing Analytics

Reflective marketing analytics is less about manipulating data to force sales, and more about understanding the human narratives behind the numbers. In taking the time to listen to these narratives, marketers can cultivate stronger relationships, drive meaningful customer engagements and, in doing so, achieve more sustainable outcomes. This chapter focuses on various strategies that marketers can employ to implement a more reflective approach in their analytics practice.

9.1. Understanding Customer Behavior Beyond Numbers

The human behavior behind clicks and conversions carries a wealth of untapped knowledge. Being mindful of these actions requires more than the absorption of data, but an interpretation of what these actions represent about the person behind the screen. Look at the statistics as a starting point for conversation. For instance, if you notice that a considerable number of users abandon their shopping carts at checkout, instead of just devising strategies to lower this rate, seek to understand what could be causing this behavior. Is the checkout process complicated? Are there any technical issues? Is the burden of additional costs such as shipping impacting the final decision? Investigating these variables can lead to a more comprehensive understanding and subsequently, more effective solutions.

9.2. Using Qualitative Data

Qualitative data is an essential tool for reflective marketing analytics. Quantitative data can tell you what is happening, but qualitative data can provide deeper insights into why it's happening. It includes anything from customer feedback, reviews, testimonials, or survey responses, to social media comments and online customer interactions. It should be analyzed in the context of the customer's journey and used to explore the 'why' and 'how' behind customer purchases.

Tools like thematic analysis can help in uncovering patterns of behavior. Natural Language Processing (NLP) algorithms can automate the process and identify sentiment, common phrases and themes from large sets of qualitative data.

9.3. Engaging in Active Social Listening

Active social listening involves monitoring digital conversations to understand what customers are saying about a brand and industry online. This goes beyond monitoring mere mentions and instead, dives into analysis of context, sentiment and intention.

Social listening tools like Brandwatch, Hootsuite, and Sprout Social can provide a platform for understanding public opinion in real time. When used with empathy and mindfulness, these tools allow marketers to understand emotions, identify trends, and detect crises before they escalate, enabling timely and sensitive responses.

9.4. Embracing Ethical Data Practices

Ethical data practices are key in showcasing respect for your customers. This involves transparency in data collection, usage and storage methods. Let customers know what data is being collected and how it will be used. A clear and accessible privacy policy goes a long way in building trust and getting consumers to respect your brand and marketing practices. Take an active role in ensuring that all data practices adhere strictly to local regulations and maintain the best interests of the customers.

9.5. Refining with A/B Testing

Continuous improvement is at the core of reflective marketing analytics. A/B testing offers a methodical approach to understanding your customers better, one variable at a time. It involves comparing two versions of a webpage, email, or other content to see which performs better. For instance, you can test different headlines or images, calls to action, or even overall layout designs. The version that generates better results informs your marketing strategies. Remember that A/B testing is not a 'one-off' process. It's an ongoing endeavor to remain relevant, responsive and aligned to changing customer needs.

9.6. Incorporating Predictive Analytics

Finally, while it's important to respect the past and respond to the present, future-casting your business is equally crucial. Predictive analytics provides detailed insights into future trends using historical data, machine learning techniques, and statistical algorithms. Tools like IBM's SPSS Modeler and DataRobot can help marketers predict future behaviors, trends, and outcomes.

However, being reflective implies that these predictions are tempered with reason and understanding from a broader context. It's essential not to over-rely on predictive models, as they can't fully account for dynamic human behavior and shifts in societal attitudes. Instead, view predictive analytics as one tool in a toolkit, providing useful but not definitive insights.

Reflective marketing analytics call for marketers to be more understanding, mindful, and focused on relationship building rather than simple transactional interactions. By focusing on these strategies, you can go beyond the confines of raw data and infuse empathy into your marketing practices, providing a foundation for more meaningful and productive customer engagements.

Chapter 10. Sustainable Success: The Long-term Impact of Mindful Marketing

In an era where businesses are searching for sustainability and longevity, mindful marketing emerges as a substantial strategy towards lasting success. As marketers, we need to steer away from short-term campaigns and one-off gimmicks to focus more on cultivating long-term relationships and fostering genuine connections with our customers. As you travel through this chapter, take note of how mindful marketing weaves into the fabric of sustainable success.

10.1. Heeding the Long-term Perspective

There's a common misconception that marketing is solely about making a sale. True marketing is much more encompassing – it's about nurturing relationships, encouraging repeat business, building a brand, and creating a dialogue with your customers. Mindful marketing can be a catalyst for long-term growth as you stay committed to understanding and empathizing with your customer's ongoing journey.

Personalization lies at the heart of this approach. By listening and gathering data, you can tailor a unique, empathetic message that resonates deeply with your customers, meeting their needs on a granular level. This doesn't mean invasion of privacy but rather understanding customers from their previous interactions and buying behavior.

10.2. Ethical Data-Driven Strategies

In the data-driven world of digital marketing, it's easy to see customers as numbers or statistics. In this reality, it can be challenging to honor the individual human aspect within the data. Mindful marketing asks us to remember that behind every data point is a person with unique needs, desires, and feelings.

The good news is it's possible to be both data-driven and mindful. The key is 'ethical responsiveness' – leveraging your customer data in ways that bring them real value without infringing on their privacy. Prioritize transparency in all your data practices and ensure data privacy measures are firmly in place. By respecting and protecting your customers' data, you promote trust and deepen your relationship with them, lending to longevity and sustainability for your brand.

10.3. The Power of Engaging Content

Elevating your content creates an incredible opportunity to engage on a deeper level with your audience. Fostering a storytelling strategy can humanize your brand, making it more relatable. Success here isn't just about the stunning visuals and catchy headlines; it lies in crafting narratives that touch your customers emotionally. By weaving your brand values and mission within your content, you reaffirm your commitment to your audience and create stronger ties with them.

When formulating your content, always ask yourself- 'Would this bring value to my customer's life?' By asking this, you ensure that your content becomes an extension of your mindful approach, adding to sustainable success.

10.4. Mindful Metrics for Sustainable Success

Metrics are the lifeblood of digital marketing, and 'Mindful Metrics' is about nurturing an approach where these numbers drive empathy and understanding. Instead of seeing metrics as mere result-oriented endpoints, they become starting points for a cycle of continuous learning and improvement.

This shift in perspective means marketers can leverage metrics to refine strategies, identify customer pain points, and fine-tune their offerings accordingly. What's more, by using these metrics, you can forecast and respond to market changes proactively rather than reactively, making you not only efficient but also resilient and sustainable.

10.5. The Impact of Mindful Marketing

Mindful marketing isn't a one-time tactic. Its implications are best seen and measured over time. However, several discernible changes begin to take form in the short run. Lower customer churn rates, increased brand loyalty, improved customer experience, and increased trust in your brand could be some of the early indications of mindful marketing working in your favor.

In the long run, mindful marketing can result in sustainable growth, increased industry credibility, and improved reputation. Most importantly, it allows for a continuous, meaningful dialogue with your customer, creating an environment that welcomes and promotes growth.

10.6. In Closing: Your Mindful Journey

Embracing mindful marketing is a journey, not a destination. It involves continuous learning, iterating, and refining your strategy. A simple mantra to remember is 'Listen, Learn, and Love.' LISTEN to your customer data, LEARN from your metrics, and LOVE the process of enhancing the customer experience.

Understanding that your customers are not just figures on a graph but individuals with a unique set of desires and needs is the beginning of this journey. By interweaving consumer data with empathy and ethical practices, you can strike a fine balance—resulting in not only sustainable success for your brand but also meaningful relationships with your audience.

Chapter 11. The Future of Marketing: A Reflective Look Ahead

In a fast-paced digital era where behavioural shifts occur abruptly, it's crucial for marketers to not only track the present, but also look ahead. Empathy, emotional intelligence, and ethical considerations will continue to rise in prominence, shaping the trajectory of digital marketing.

11.1. Responding to Rapid Technological Change

Step into the future of marketing with a keen eye on rapid technological progress. The rate of new technology creation and adoption is unparalleled. Social media sites bubble up, and trends emerge overnight. As AI and automation take the reins of many facets of marketing, how do we ensure that the human element isn't lost in the process?

While automation has demonstrated a unique value proposition in terms of convenience and scale, it cannot replace the indelible human touch. The future of marketing should meld technology-driven insights with human intuition to generate lasting, meaningful customer relations.

11.2. Data: The Cornerstone of Future Marketing

Data, in its raw form, is merely a collection of facts and figures. It isn't until marketers assign meaning and context to these numbers that they become noteworthy. More importantly, as we move forward, marketers will need to fine-tune how they interpret and synthesize data.

Moving away from surface-level metrics like clicks and impressions, the future sees a focus on 'deep data'— valuing the quality of data and the stories it tells over mere quantity.

11.3. More Focus on Ethical Responsiveness

The emphasis on ethical marketing practices is set to rise in the near future. We've already seen some significant shifts in privacy laws with GDPR in Europe. The challenge lies in balancing the desire for personalized marketing with respect for user privacy. It's not just about avoiding legal issues, but about building trust with consumers.

The future marketer will leverage data mindfully, ensuring the customer's comfort and trust while also pursuing the brand's objectives.

11.4. Building Authentic Connections

In an era dominated by technology, authentic human connections stand out. Future marketing will be less about constant promotion and more about nurturing these relationships.

Storytelling will become a fundamental marketing tool, with brands leaning on narratives to communicate their values. Emotionally resonant stories invites consumers to participate, fostering connections that transcend simple transactions.

11.5. Integrating AI and Machine Learning

Artificial intelligence and machine learning are poised to take center stage in the future of marketing. They can provide invaluable insights, recognize patterns, and automate tasks - however, they should not replace a marketer's role but instead facilitate their work.

By understanding and directing these tools, a mindful marketer can leverage them while also maintaining an empathetic approach.

11.6. Balancing Personalization and Privacy

Personalization is crucial for targeted marketing but must be balanced against privacy concerns. The future will see businesses creating personalized experiences but in a way that respects consumer privacy rights and concerns.

Businesses that can strike this balance effectively will be those that prosper in the customer-centric environment of the future.

The future of marketing is dynamic and undoubtedly holds several more advances. By maintaining a focus on ethical, empathetic and mindful practices, marketers can adapt to these changes and harness the power of emerging technologies without sacrificing the human connection central to their role.